I0478018

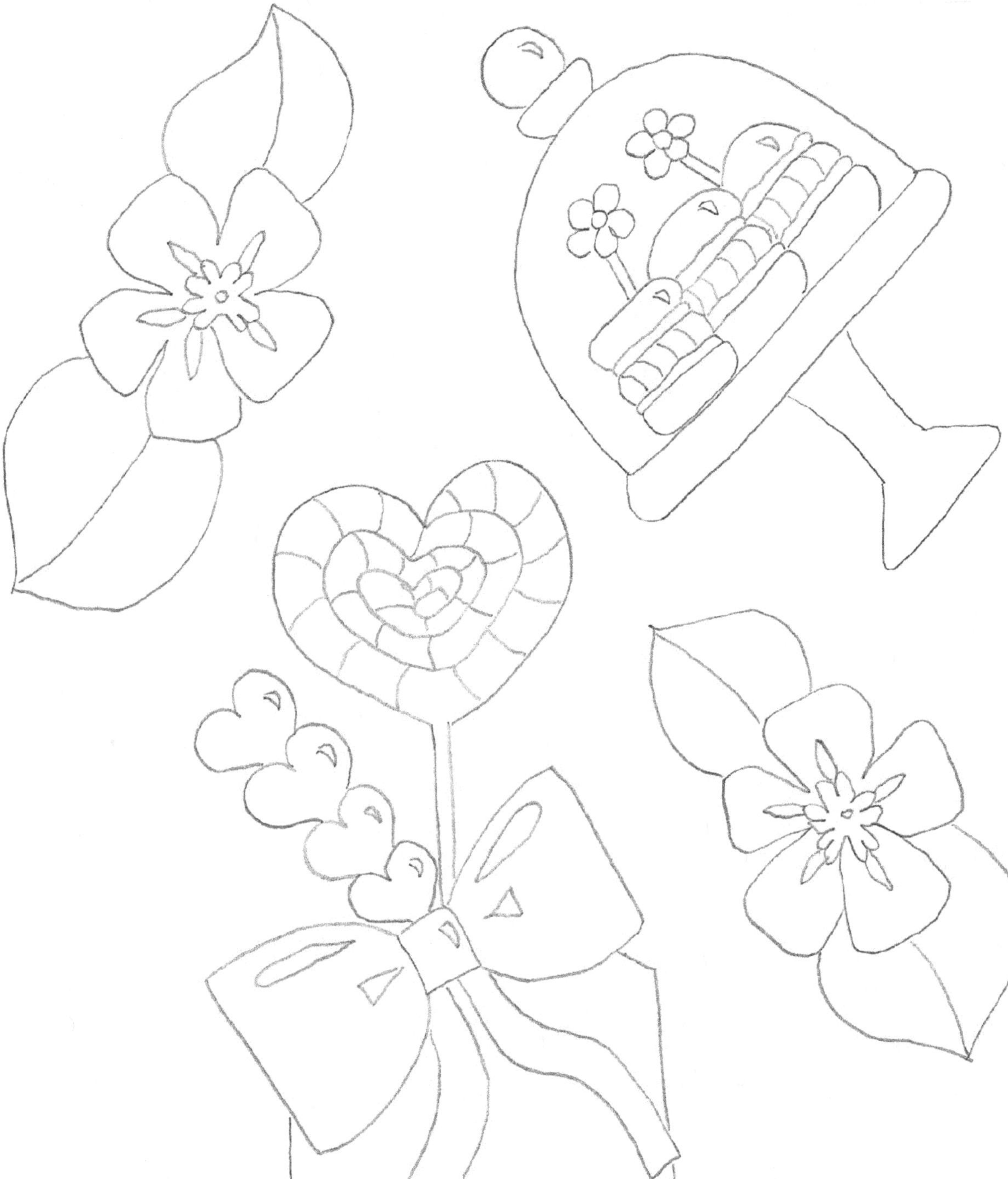

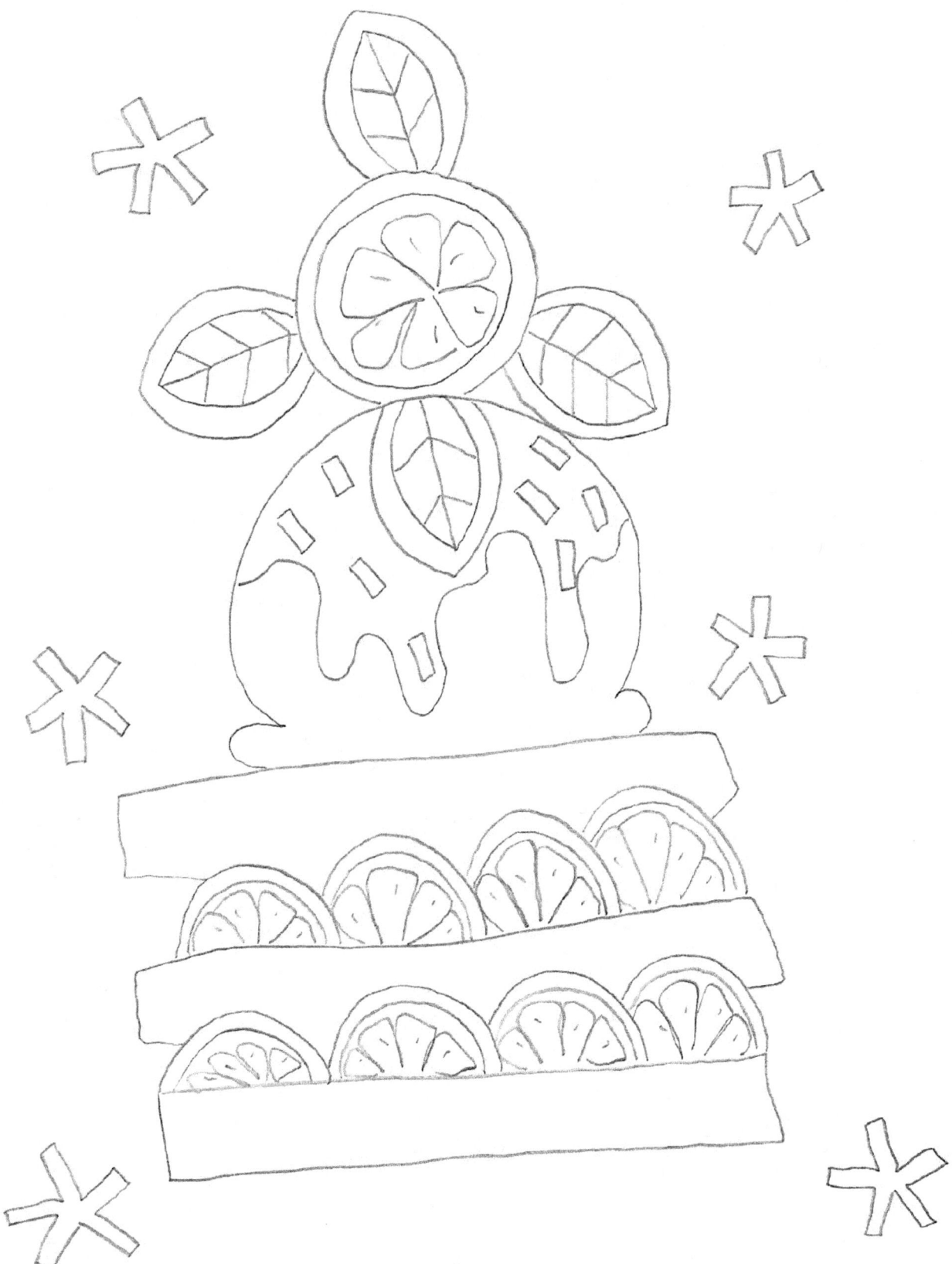

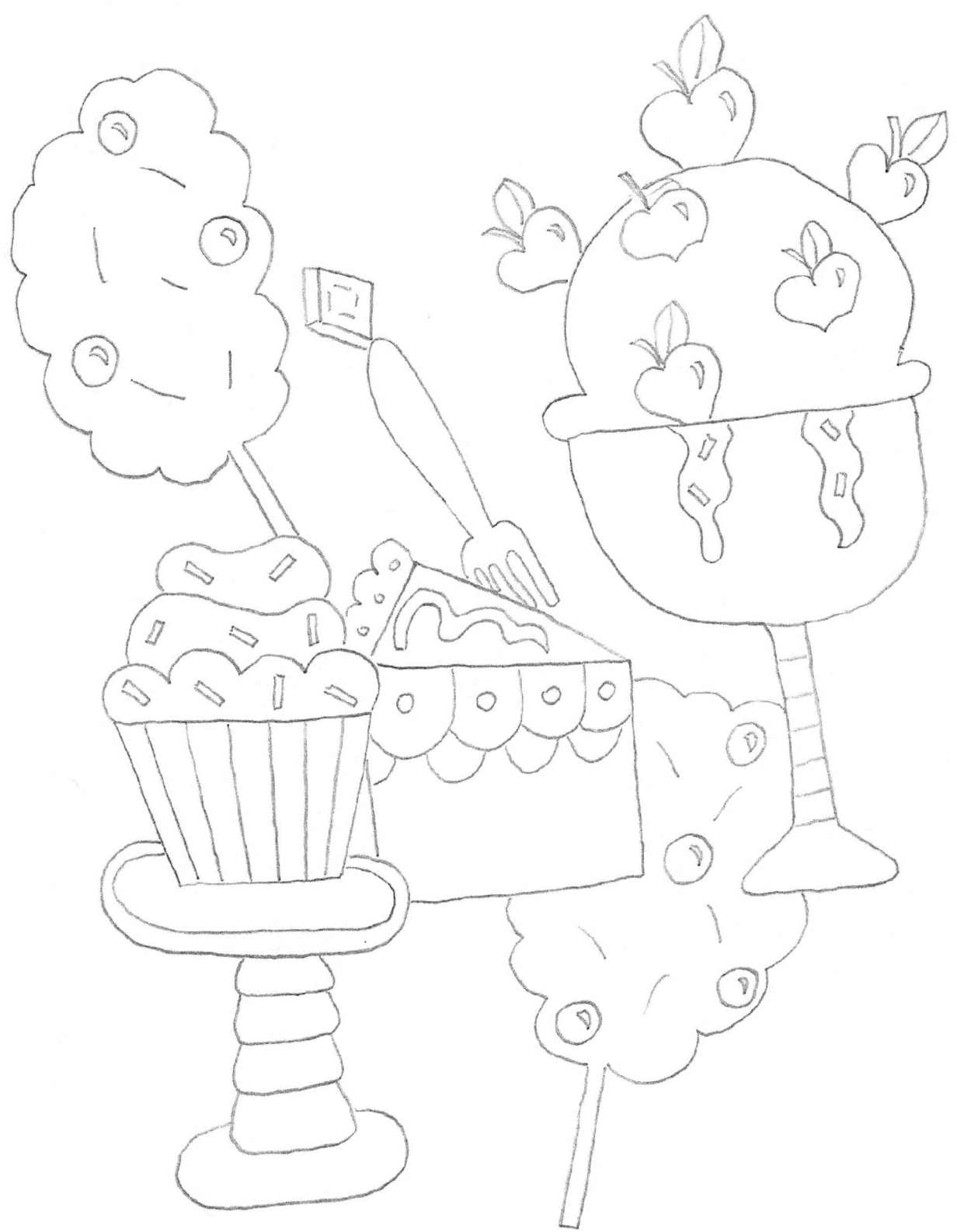

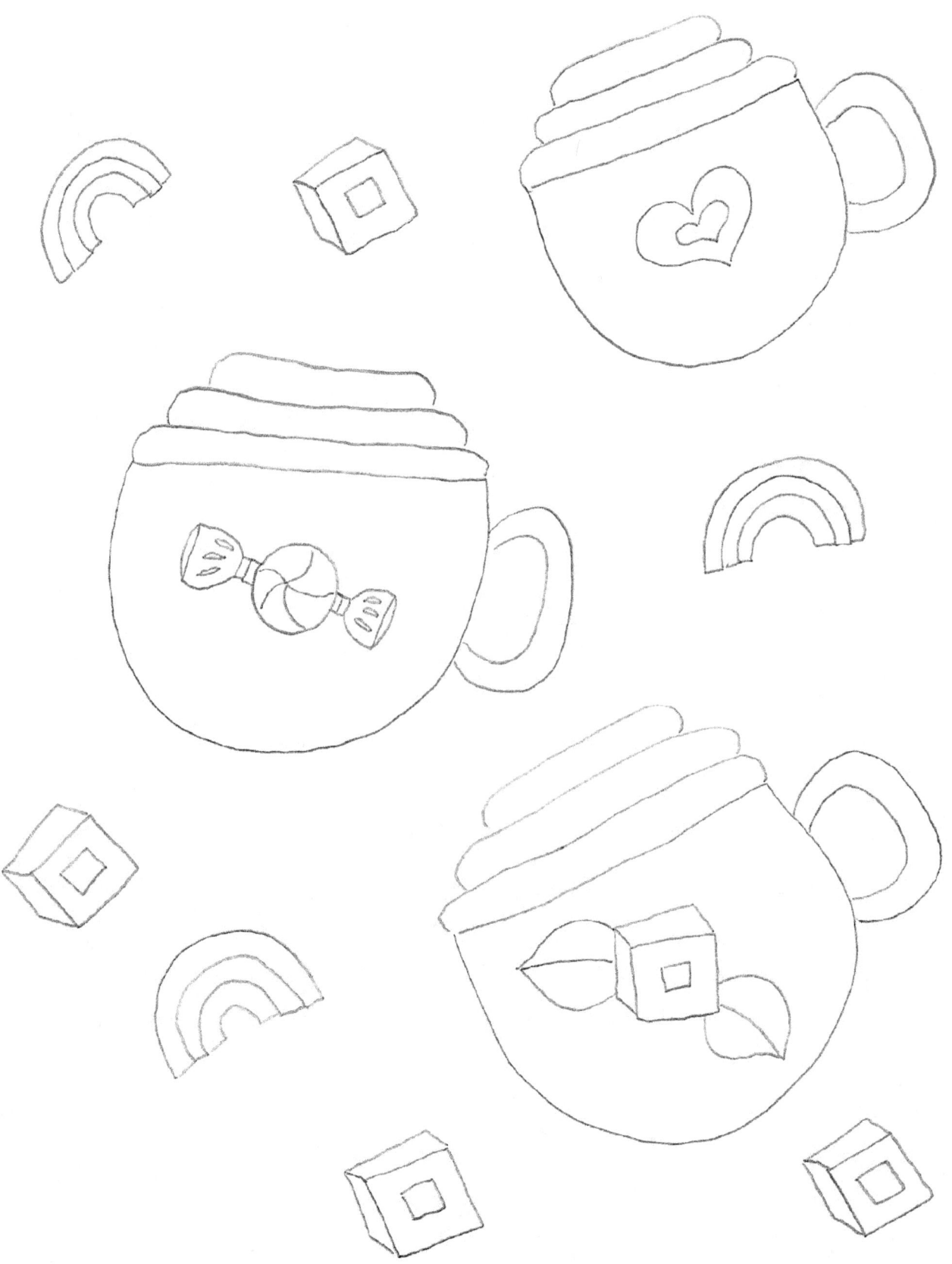

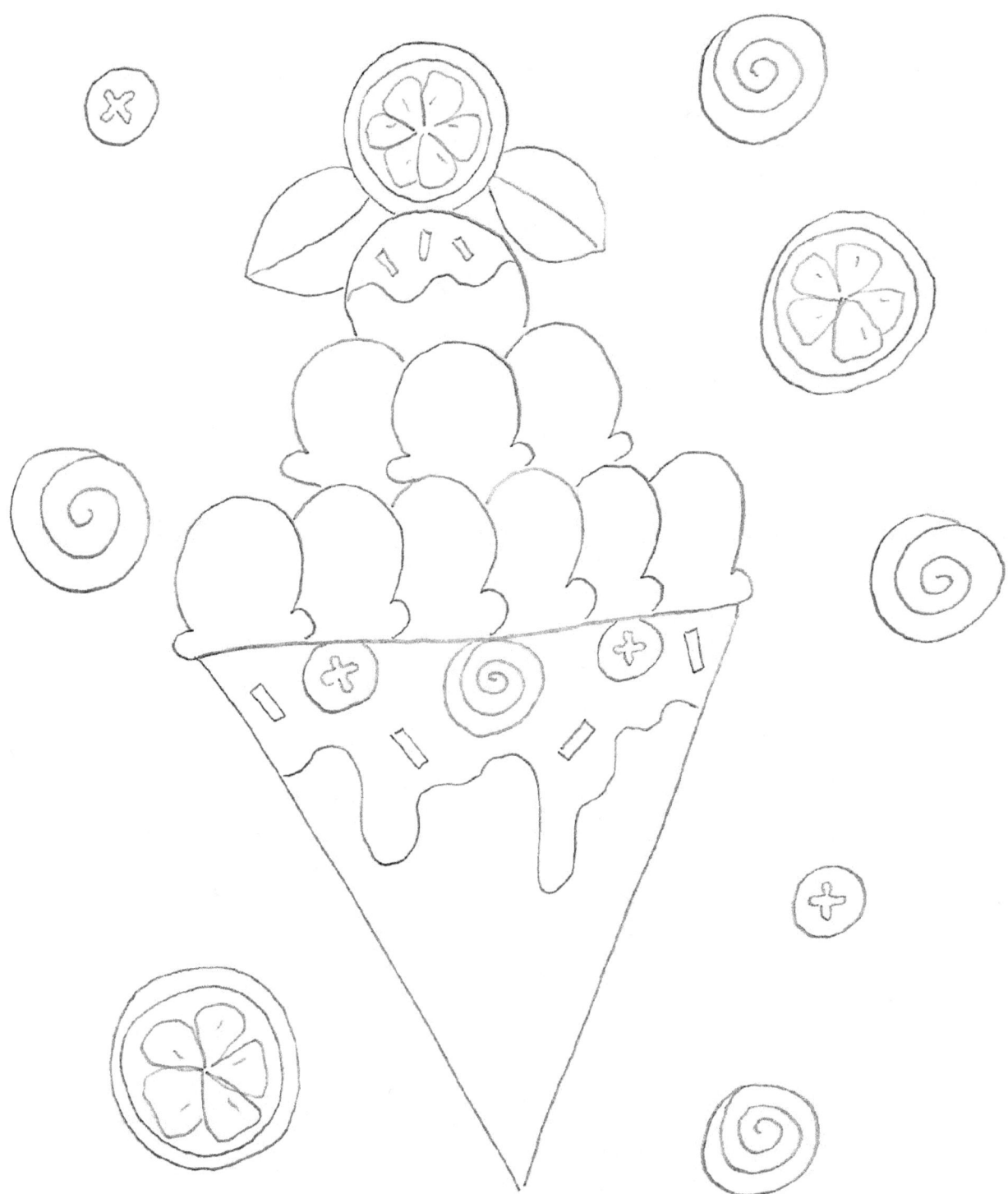

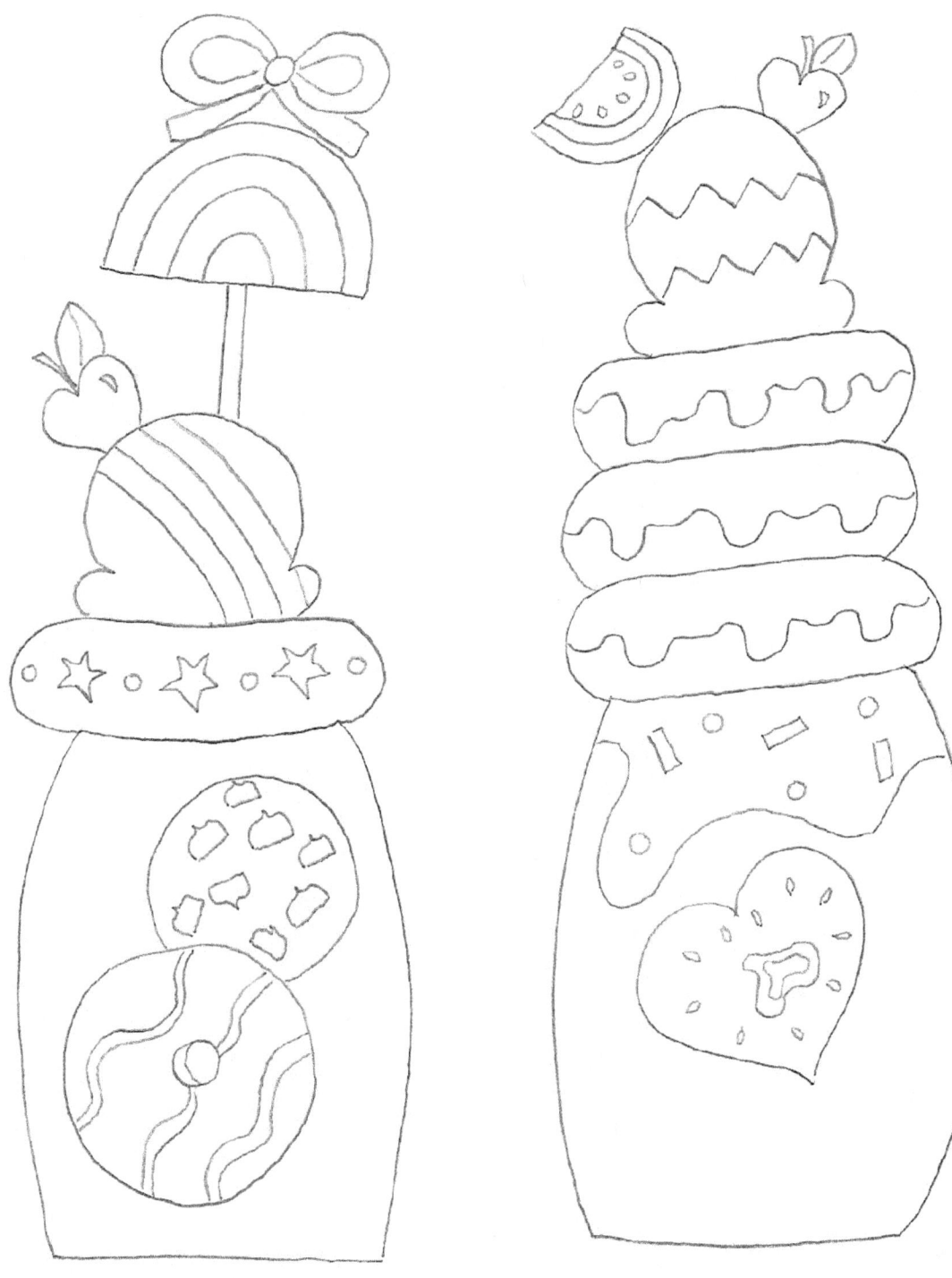

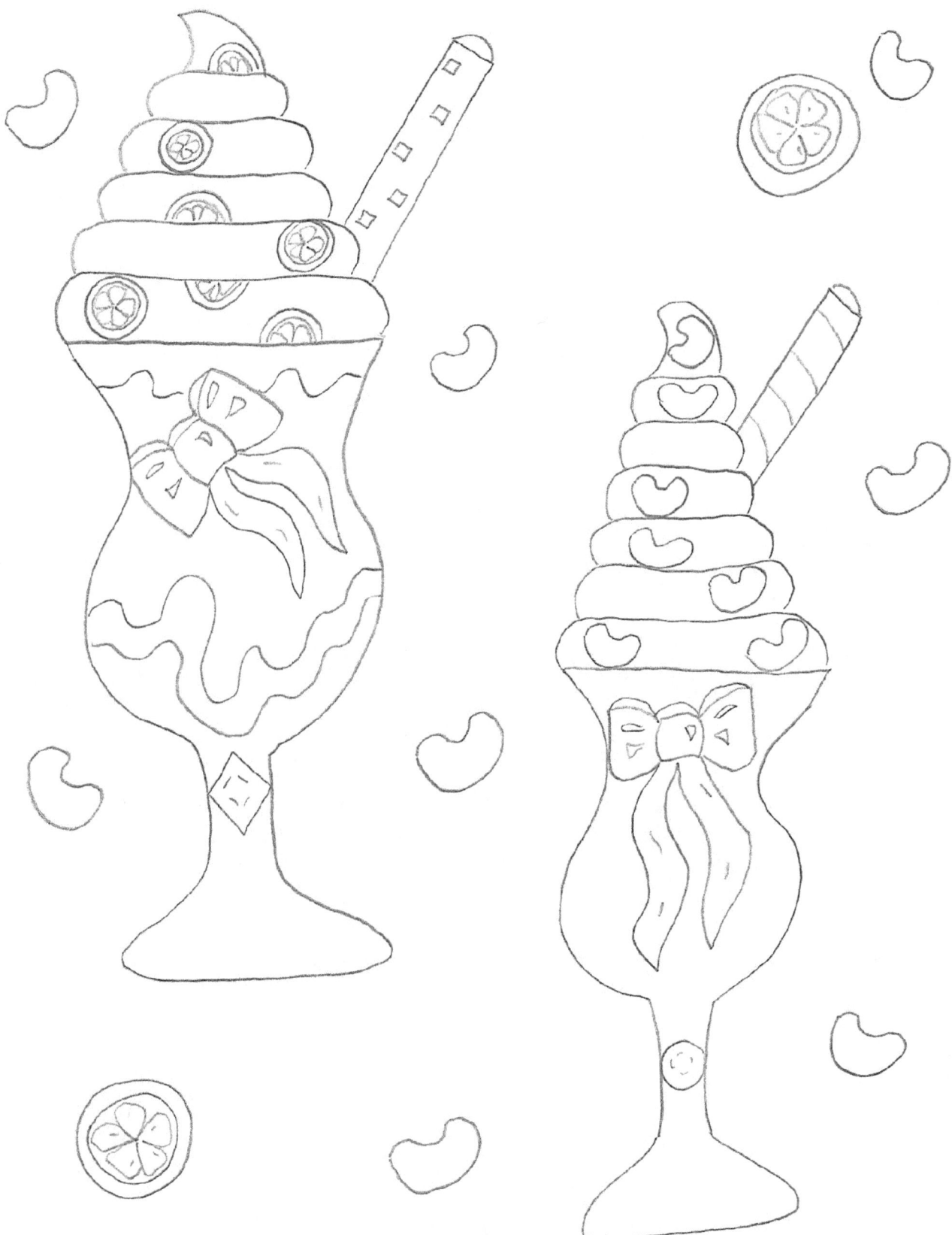

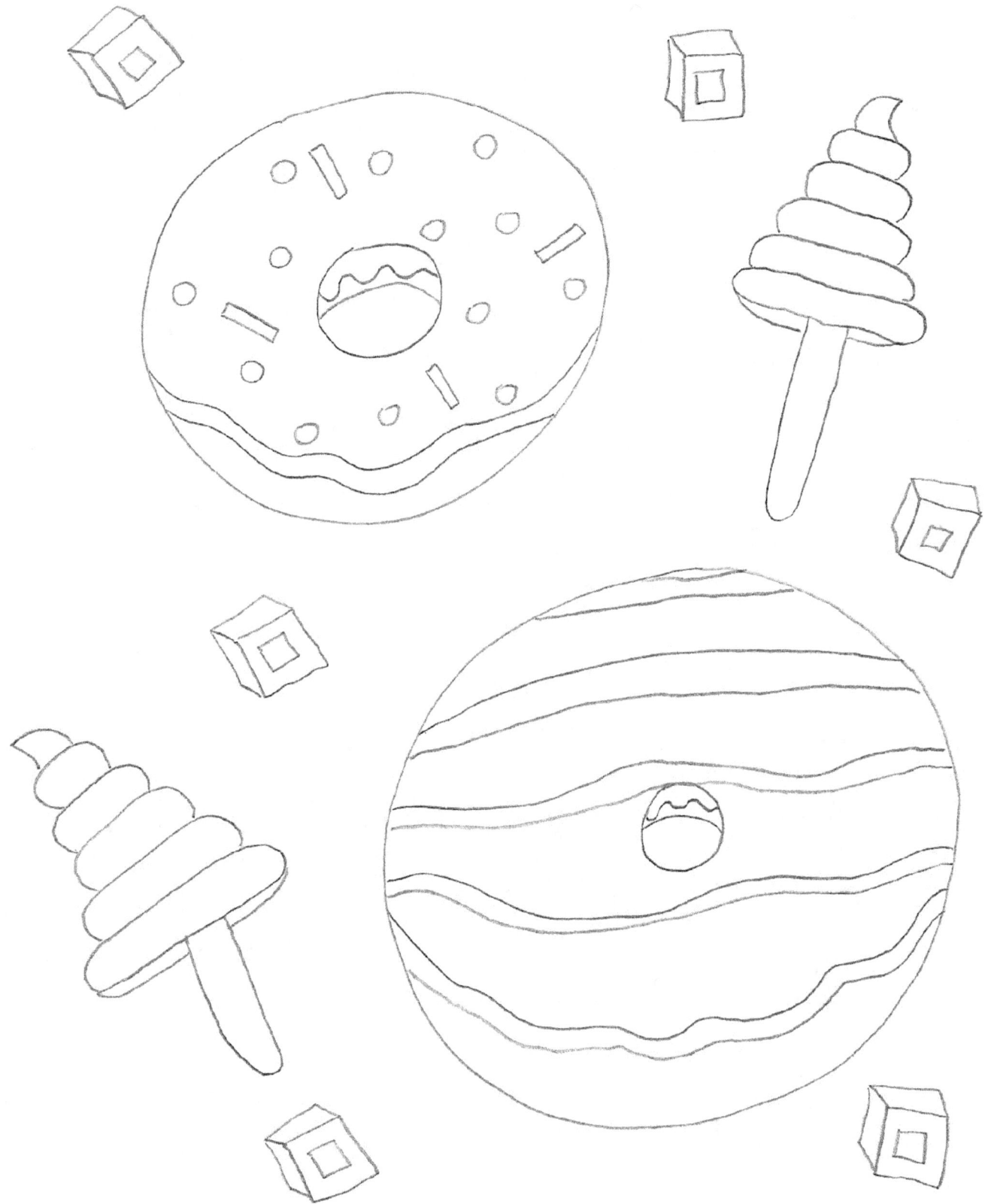

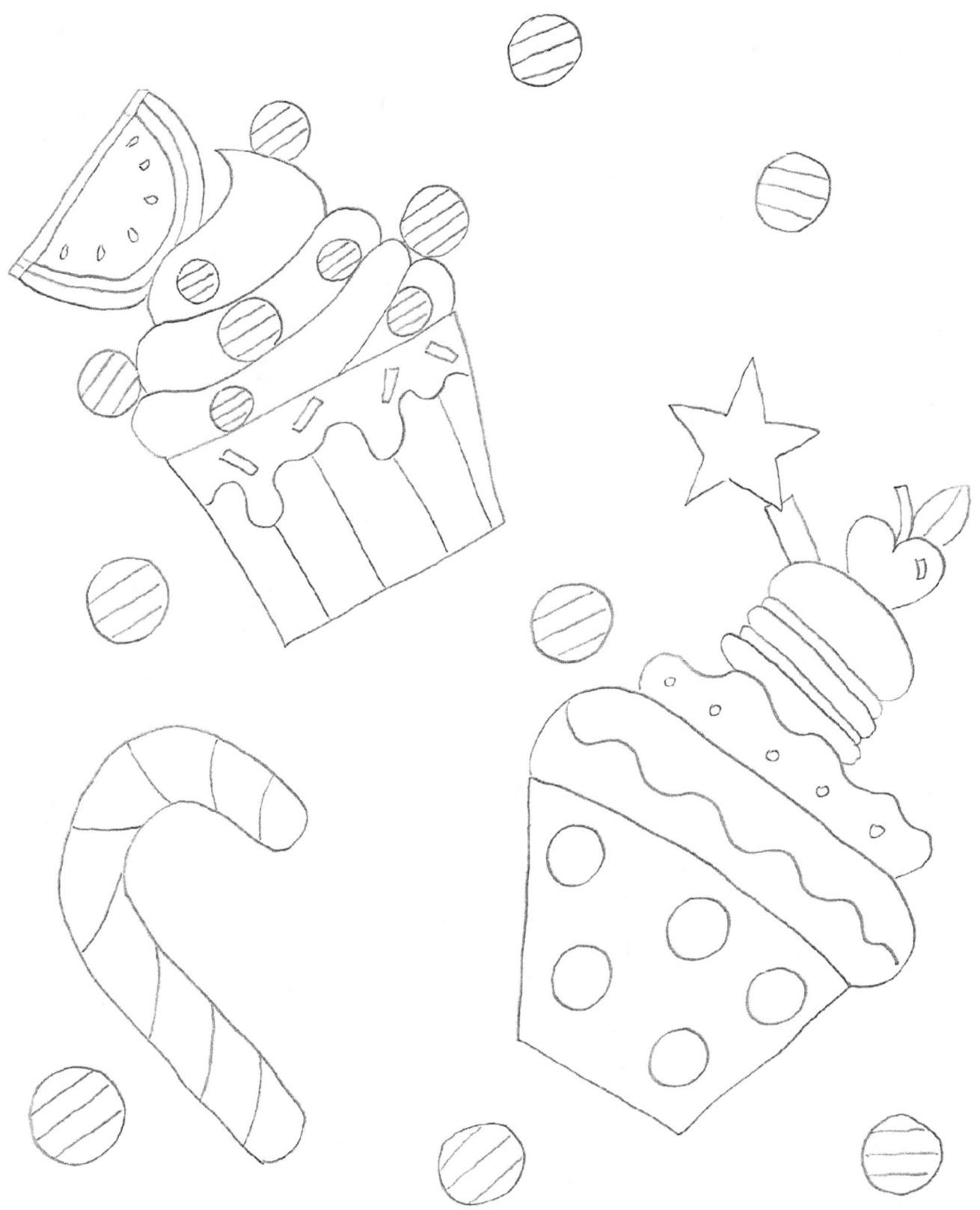

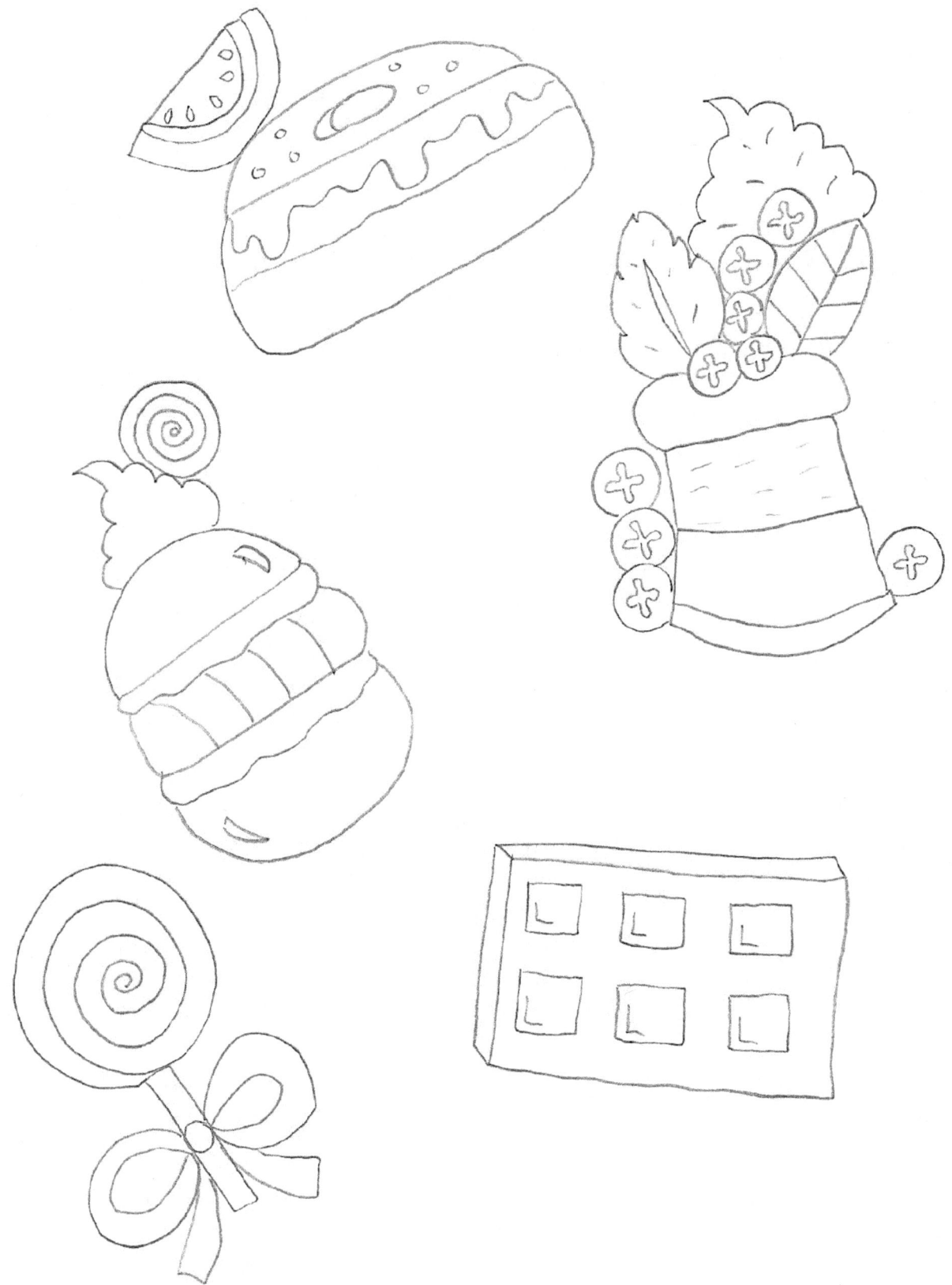

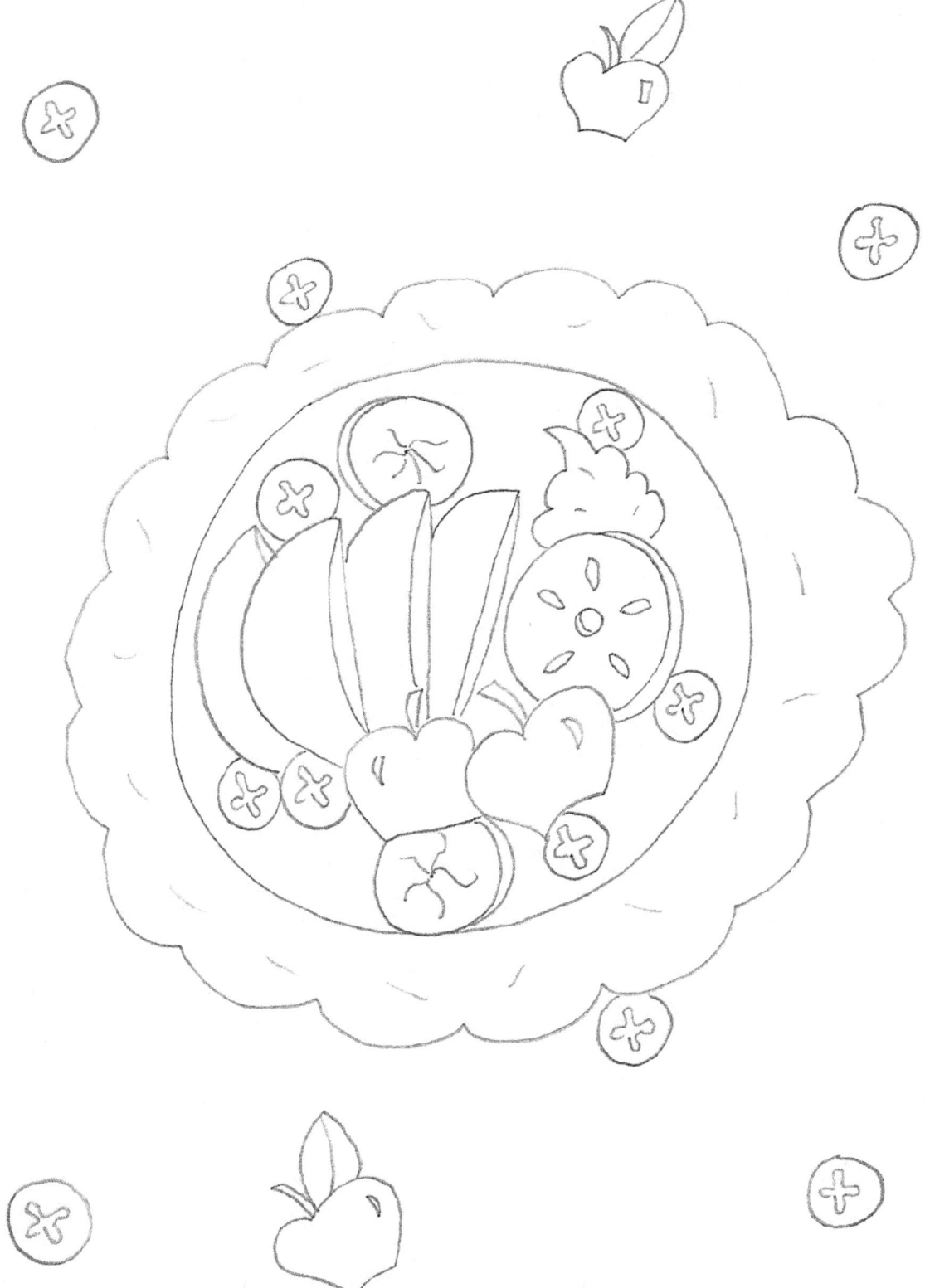

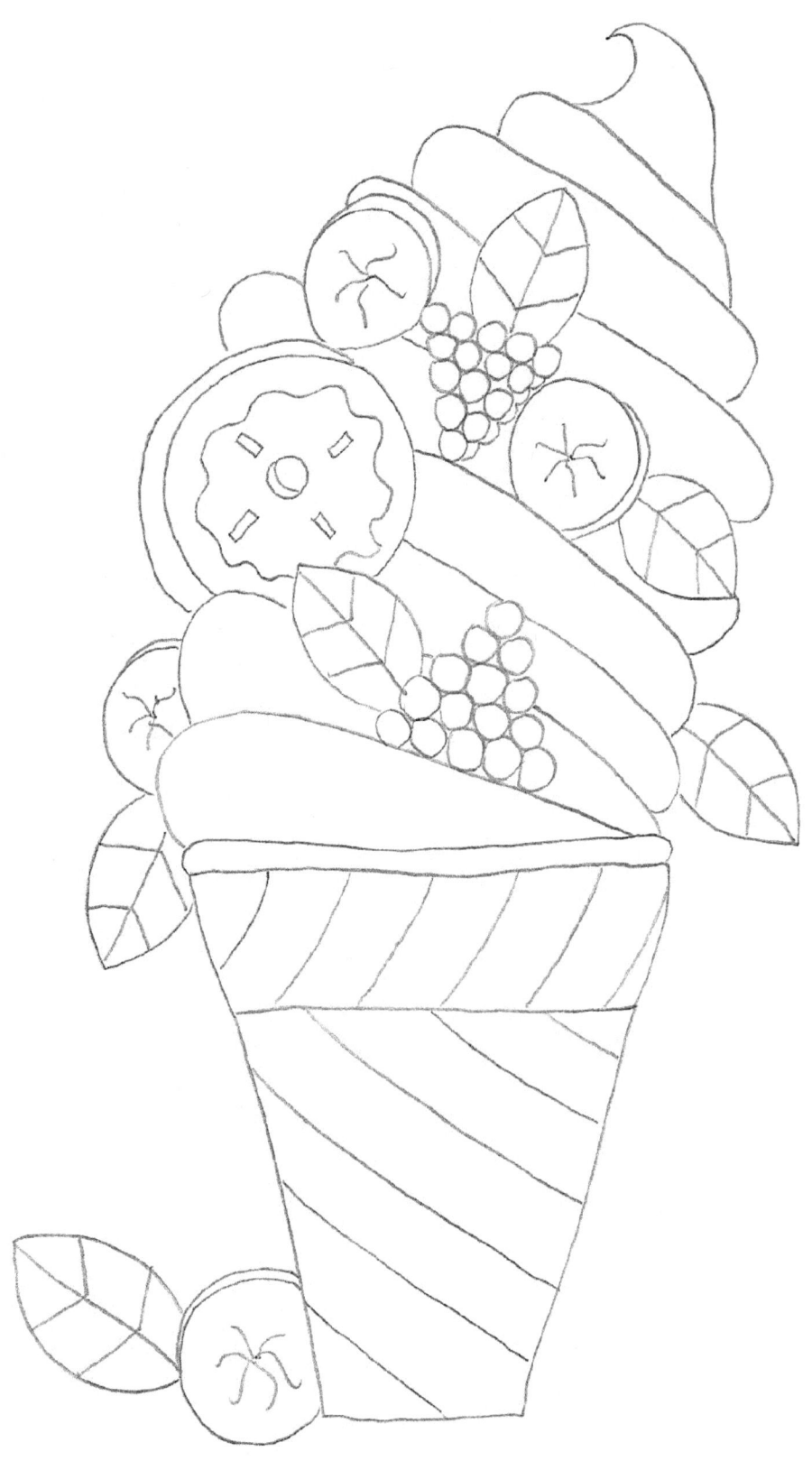

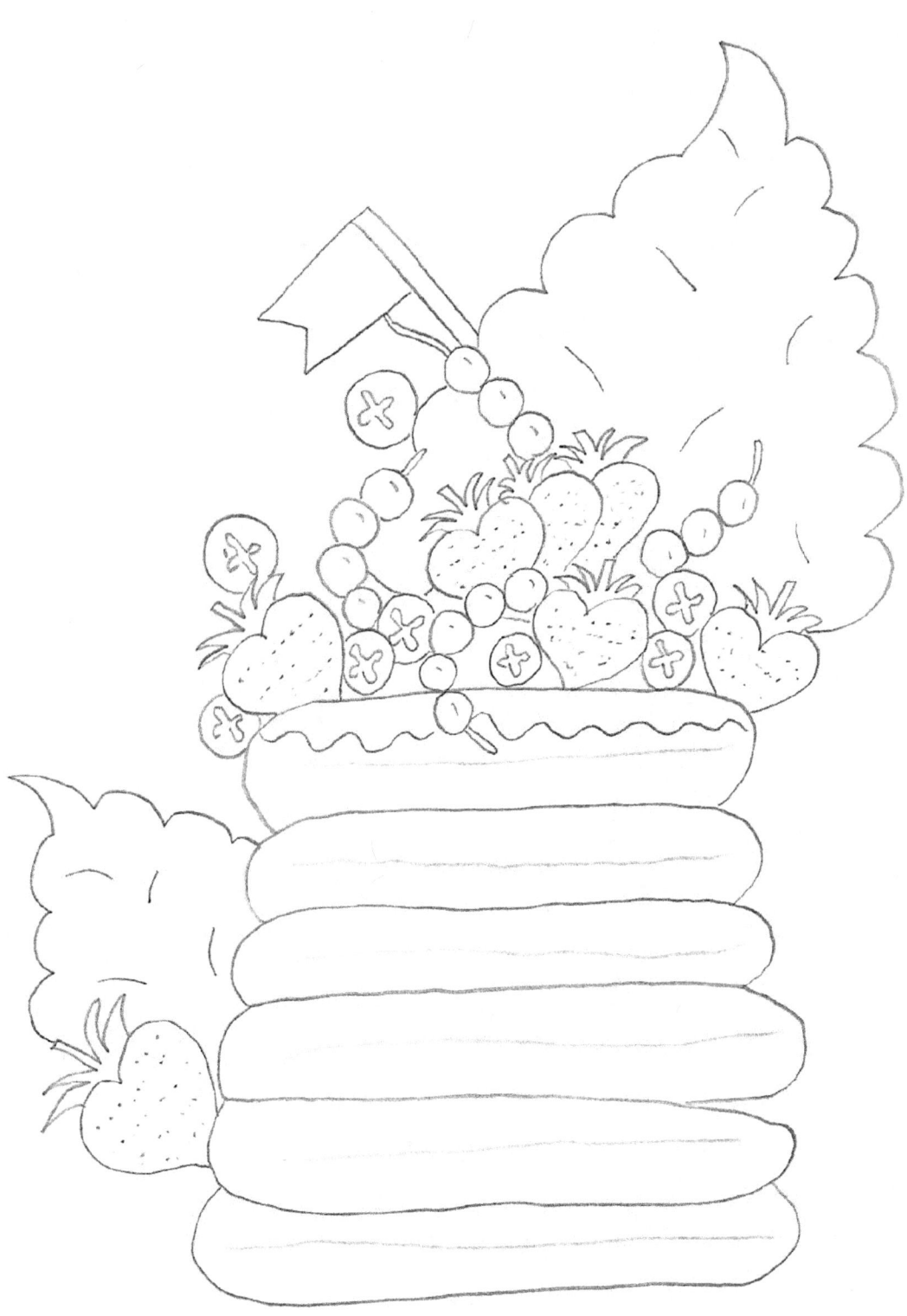

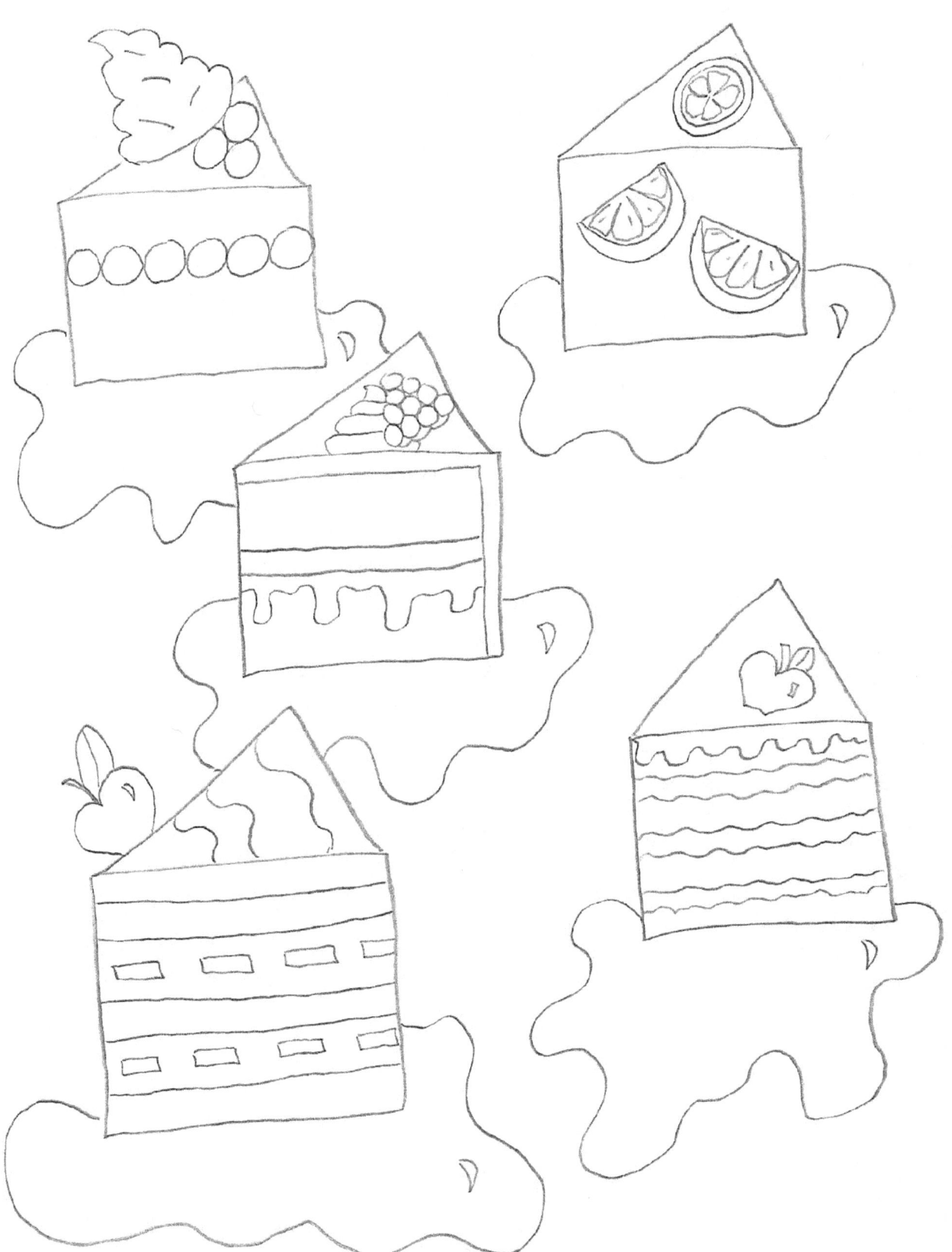

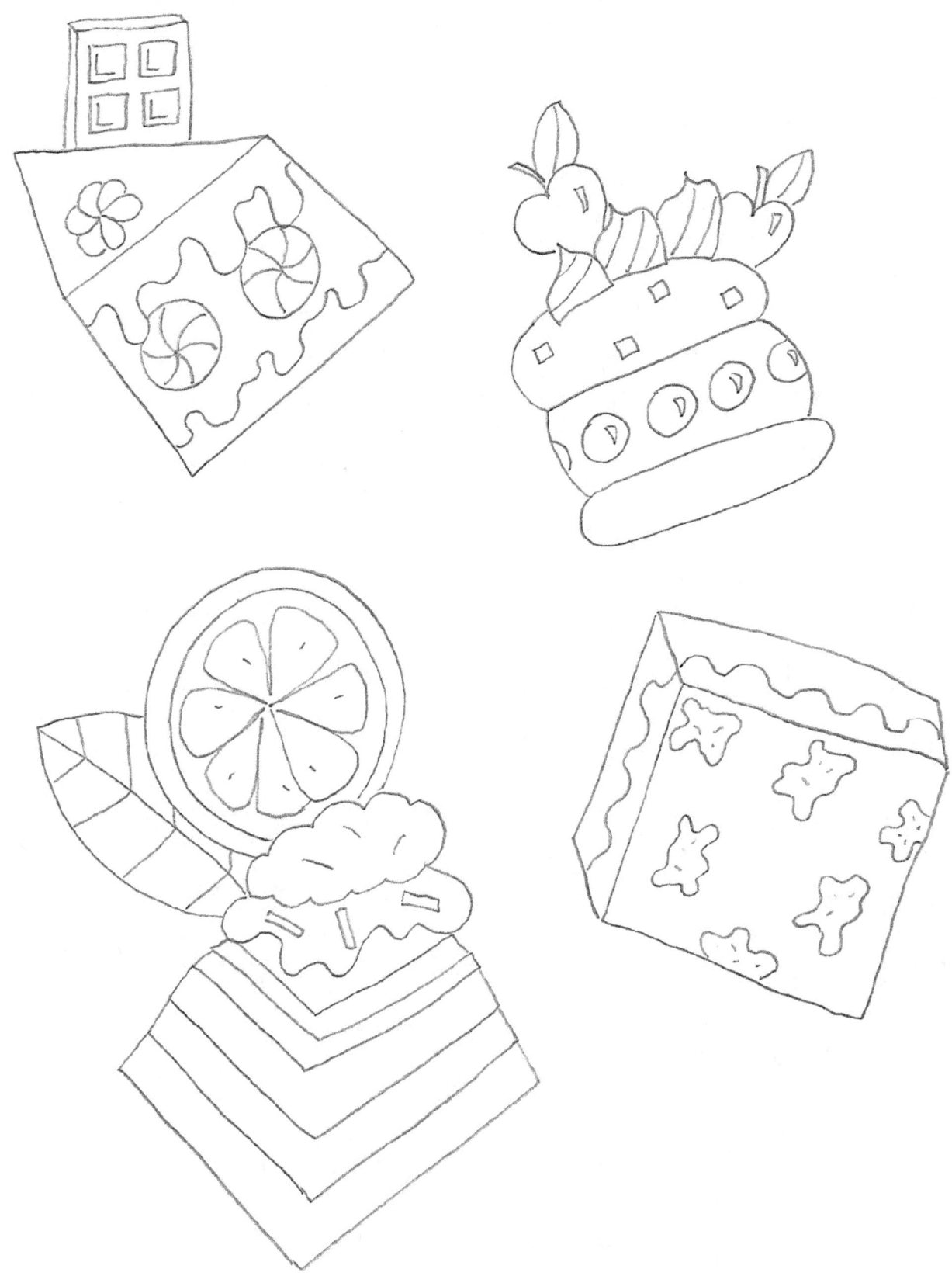

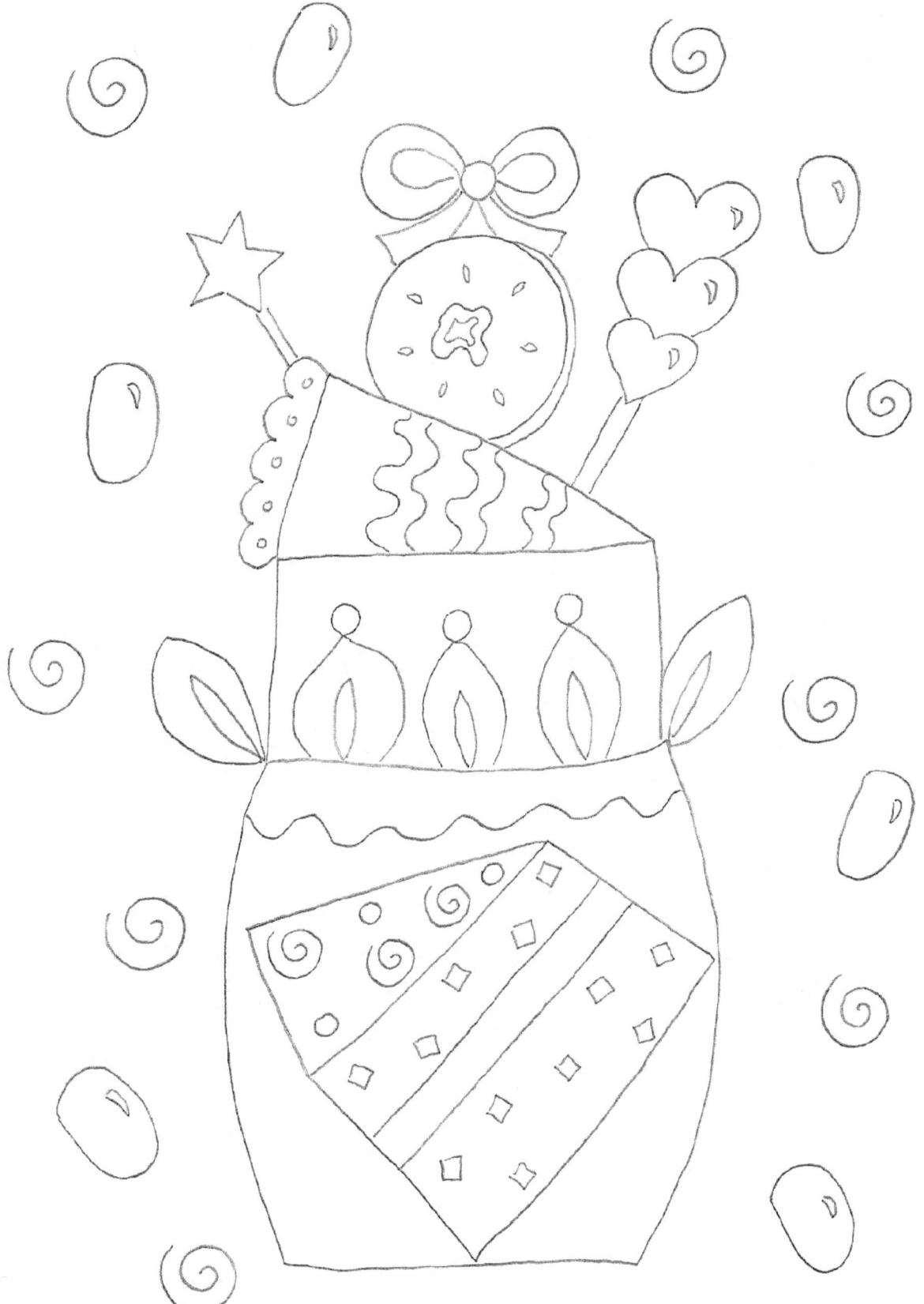

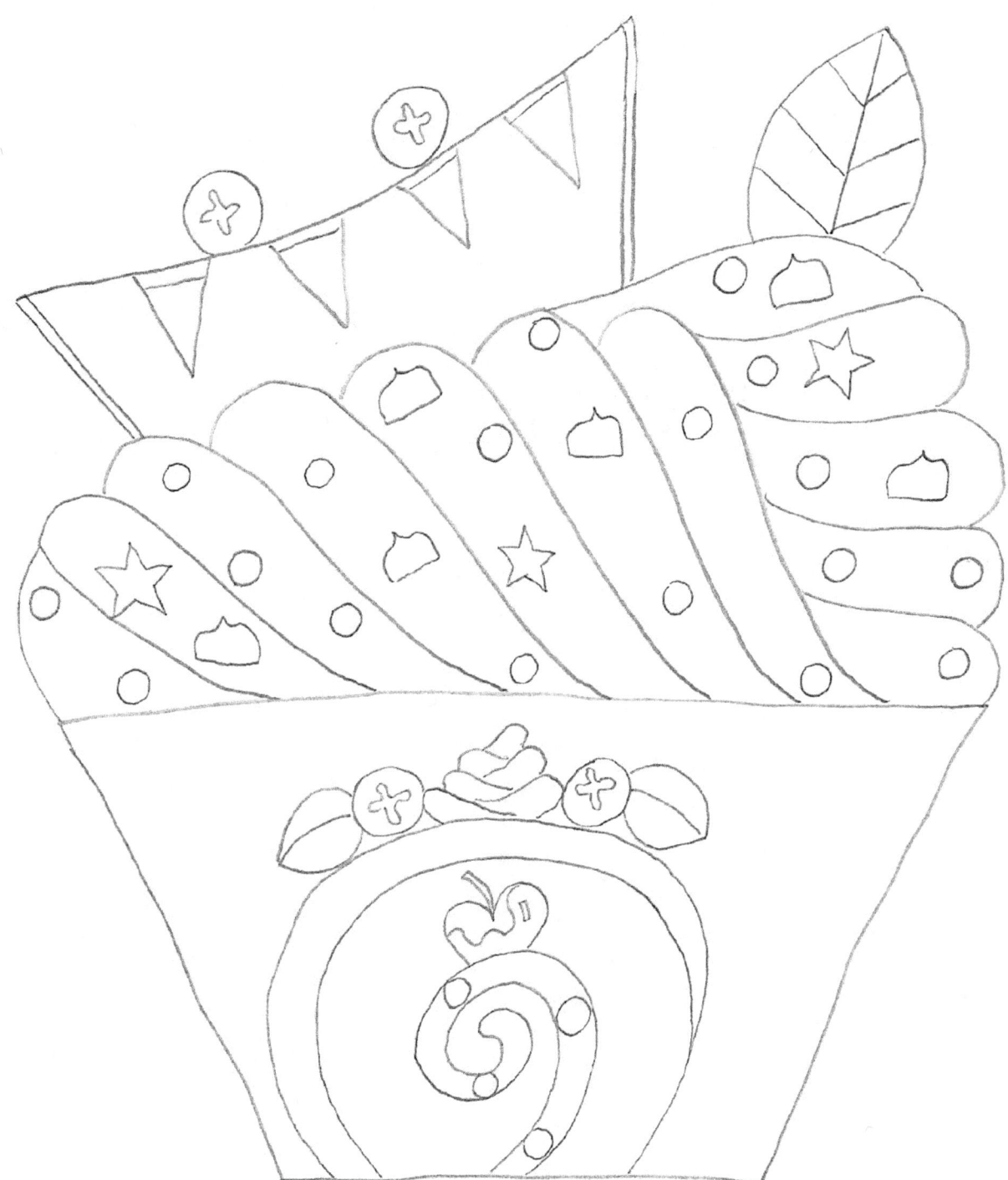

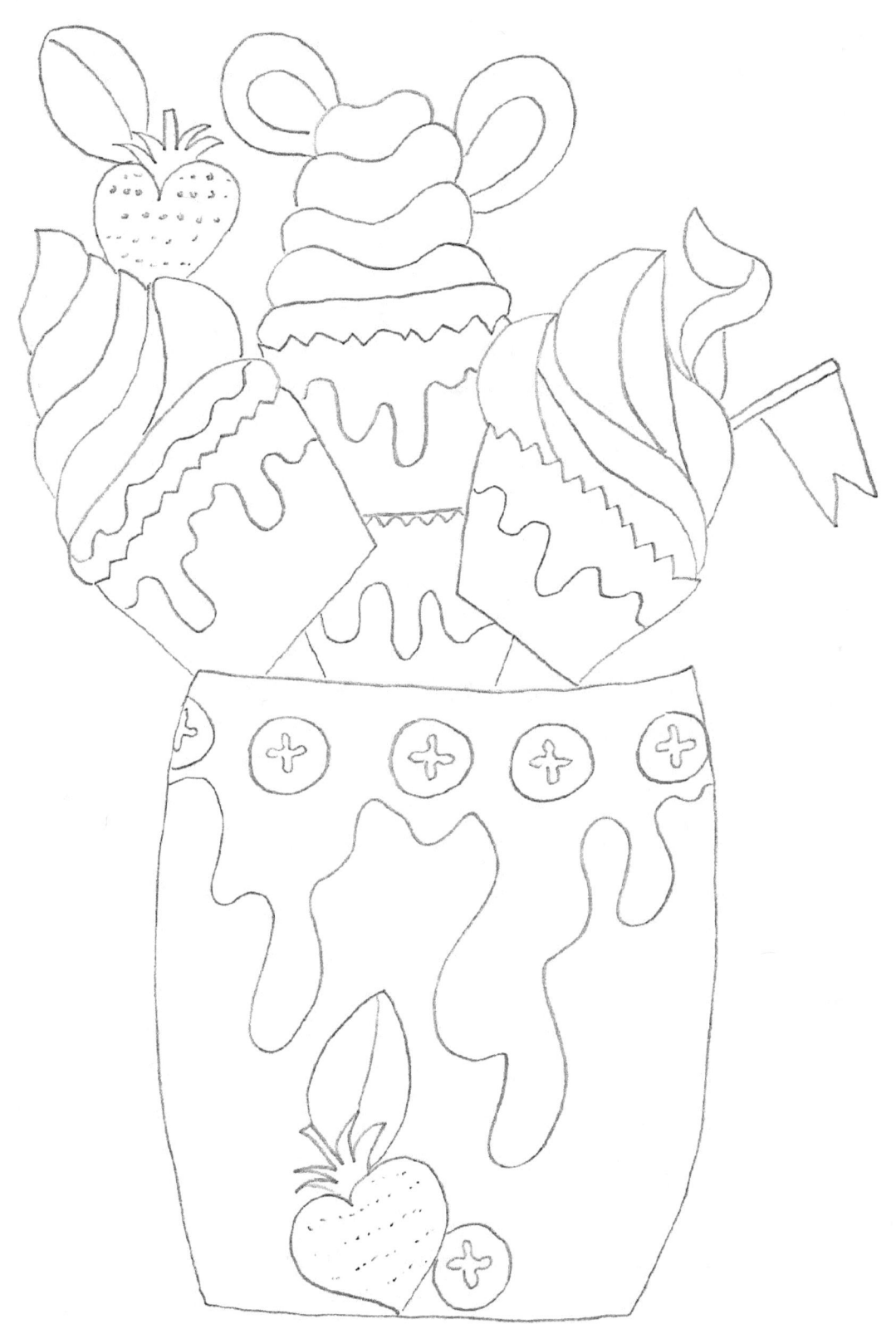

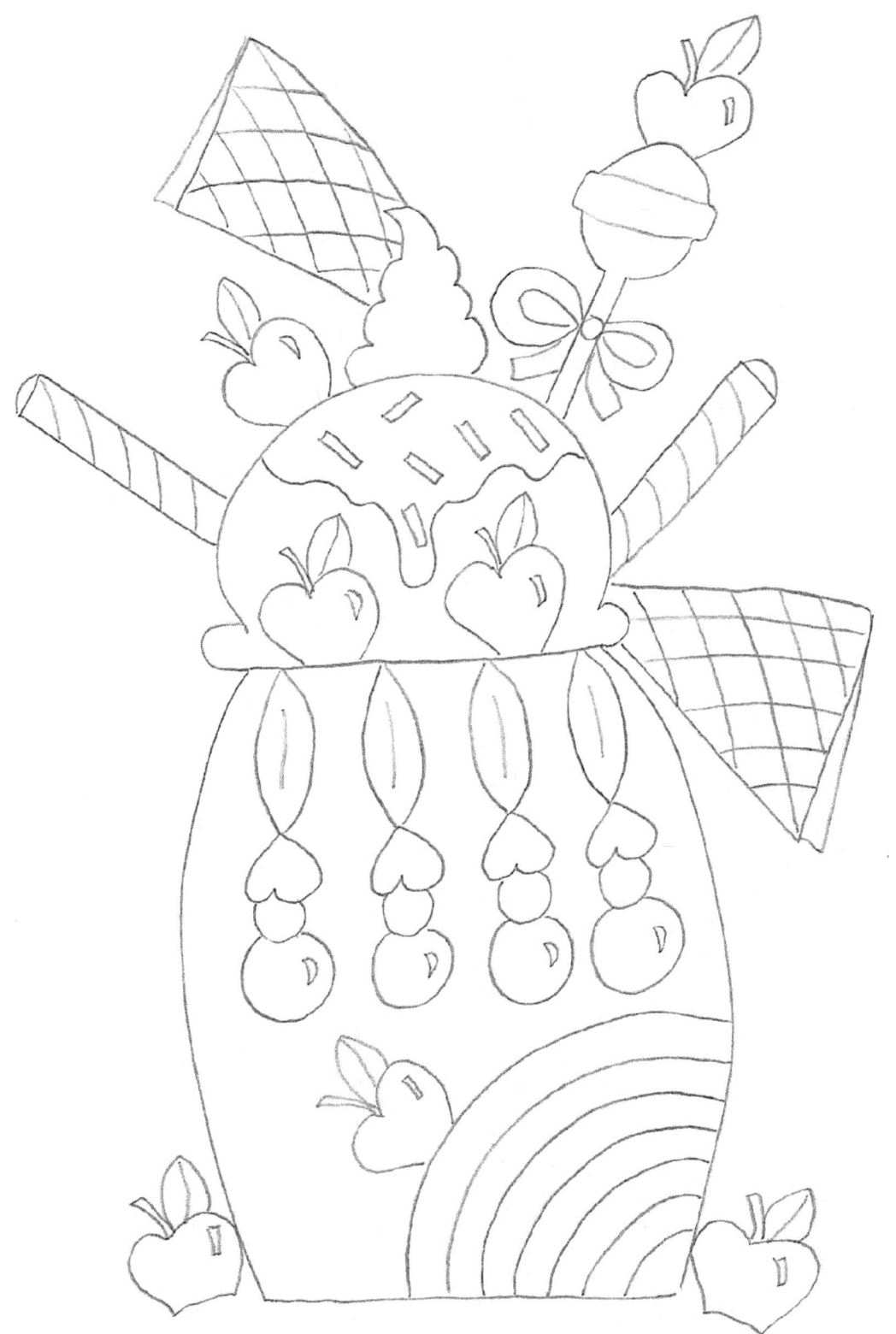

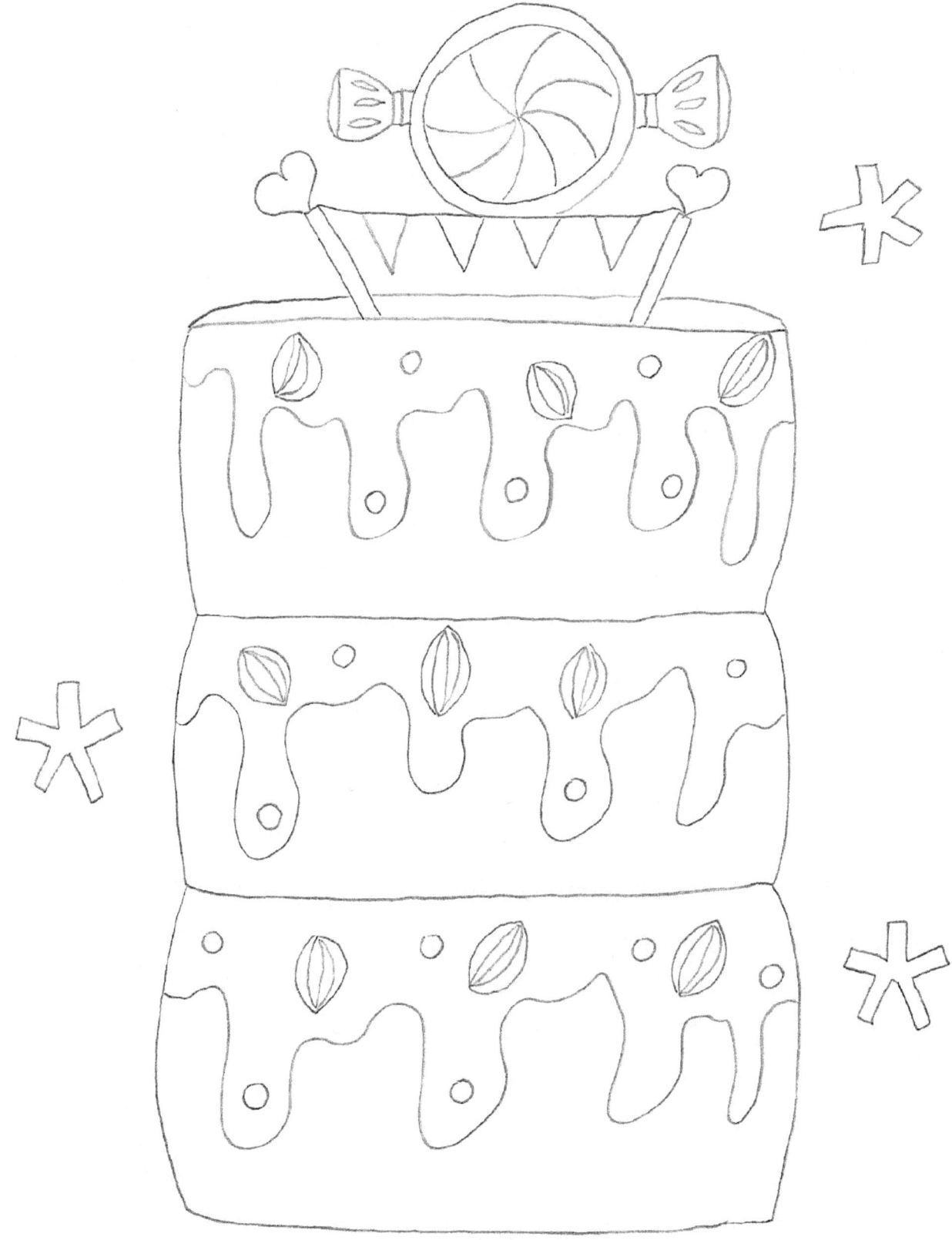

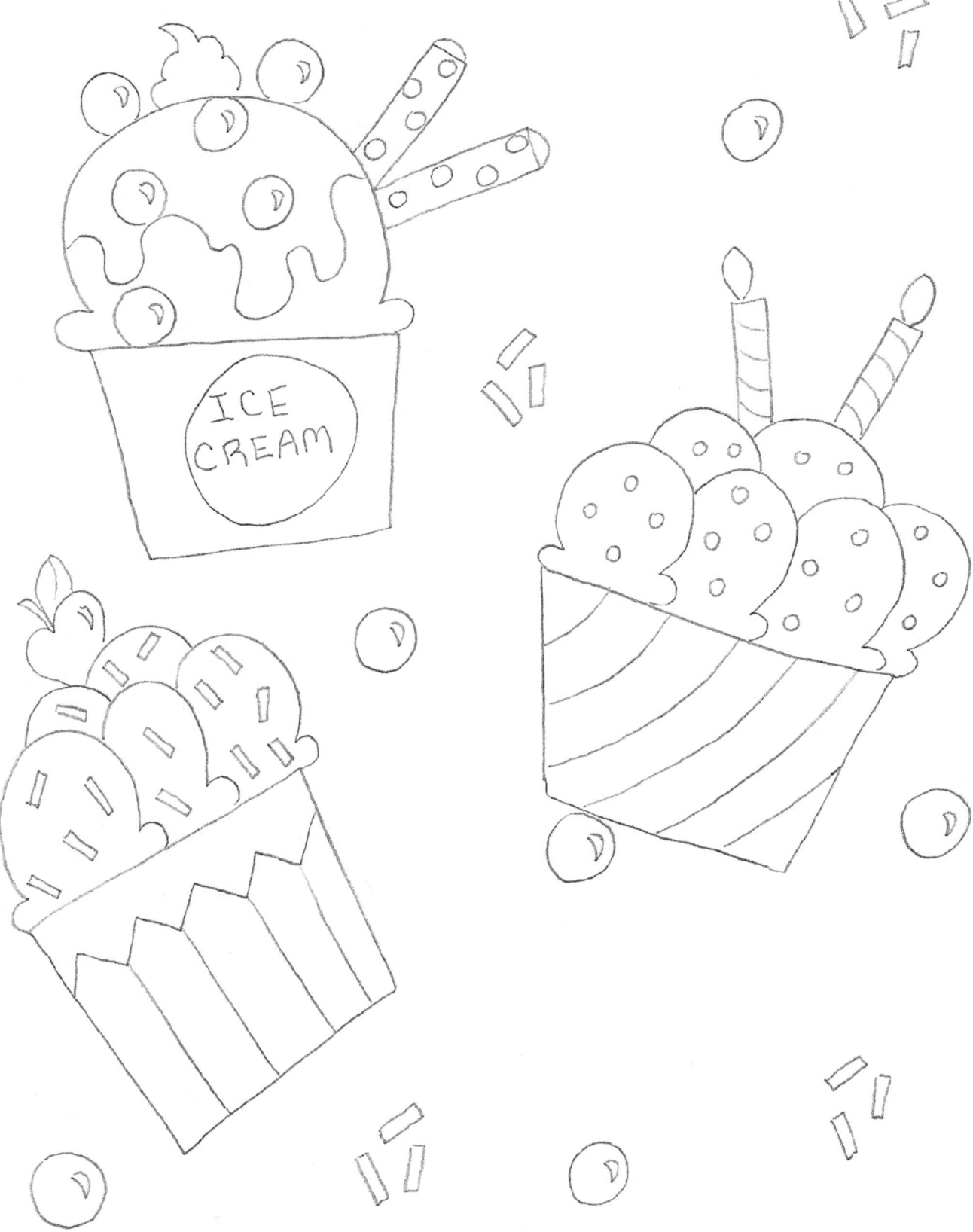

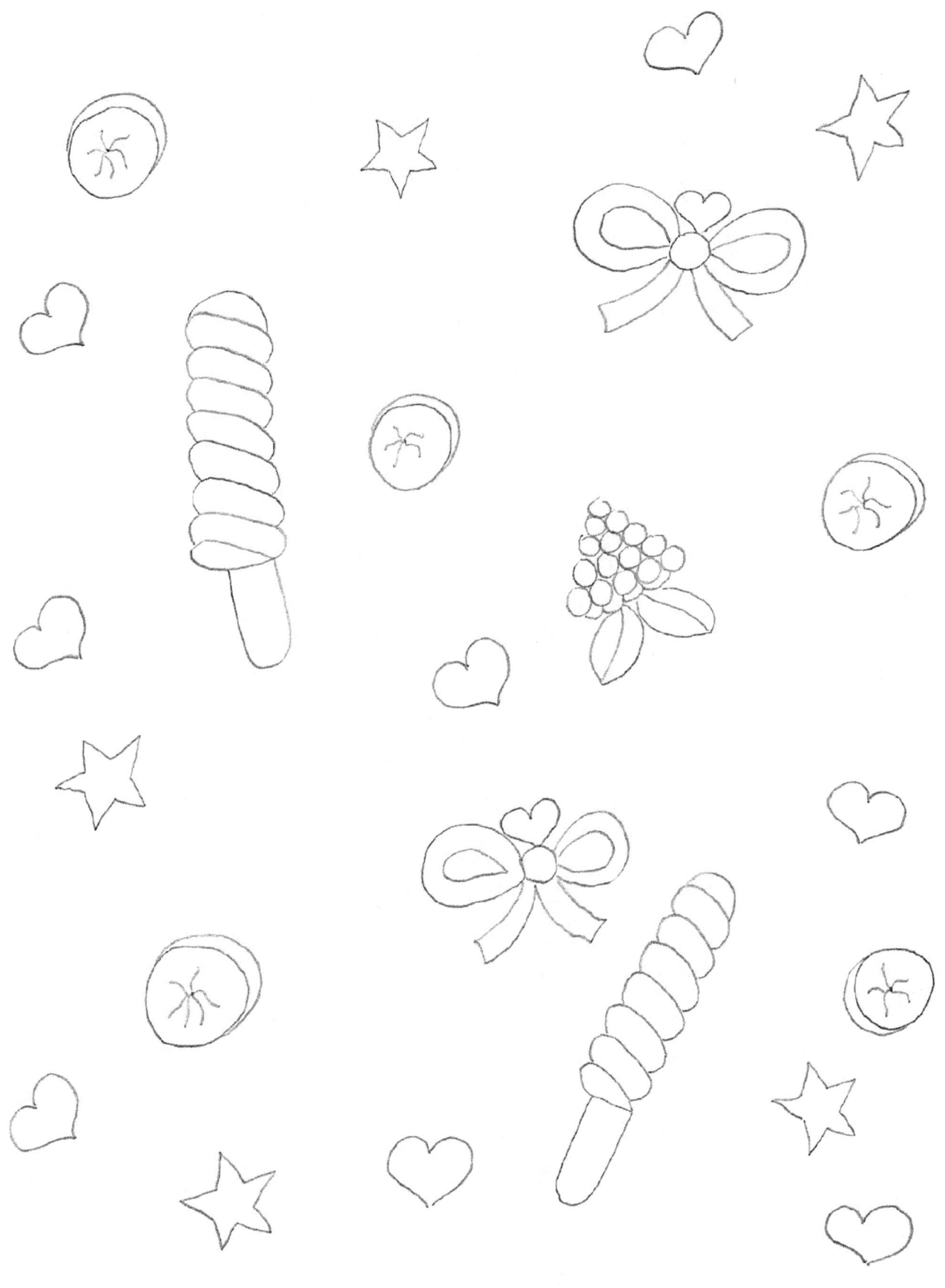

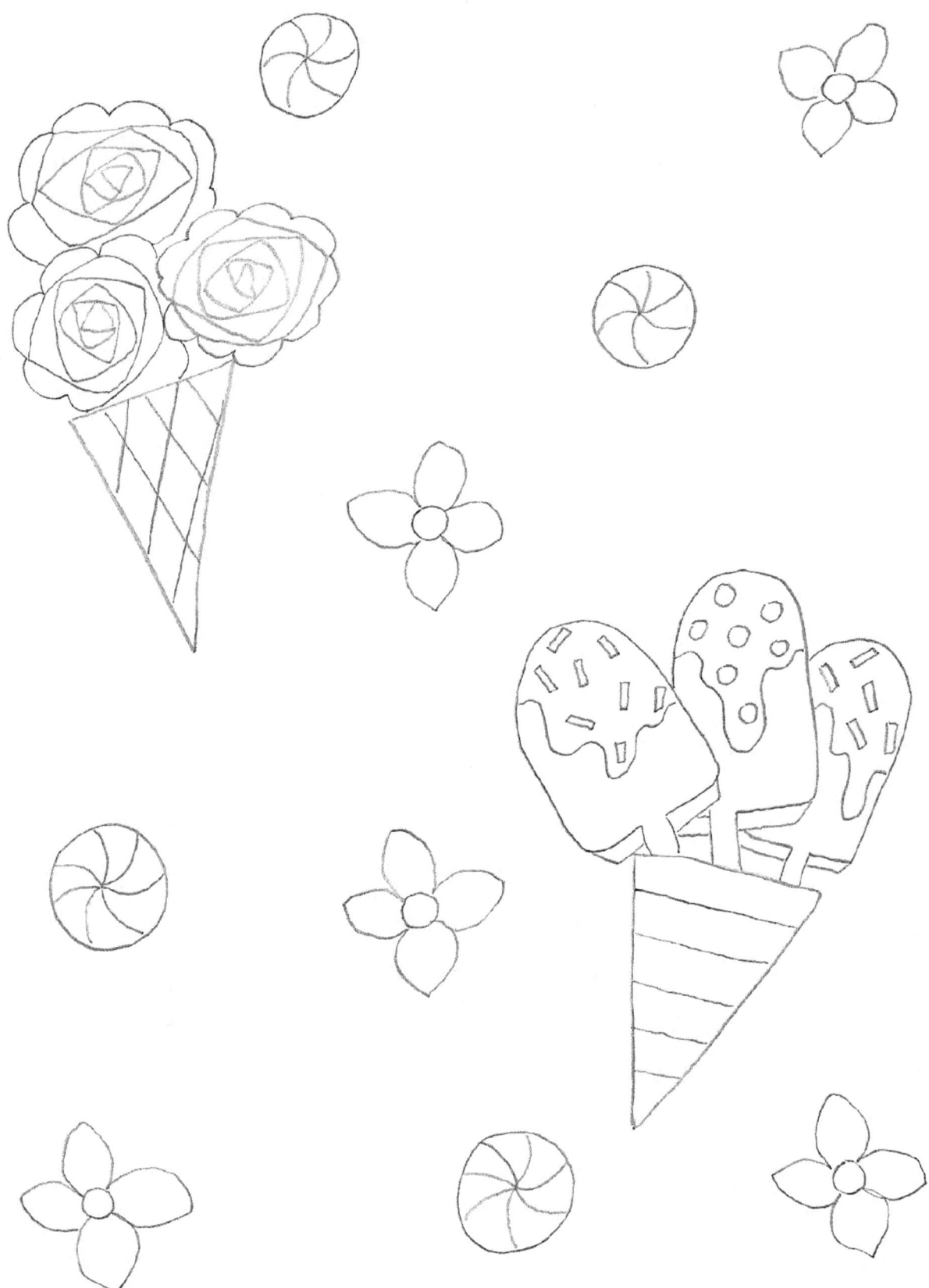

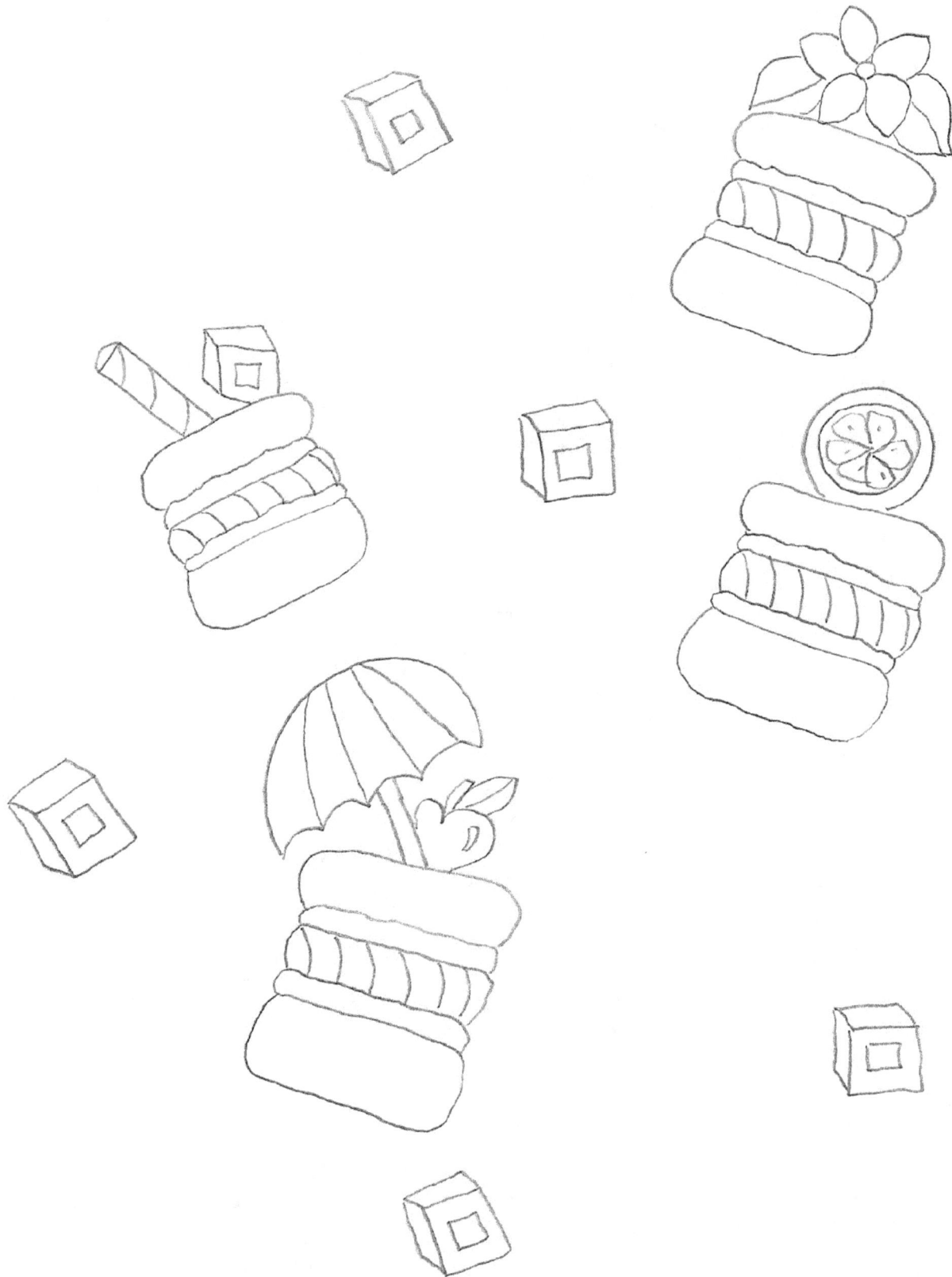

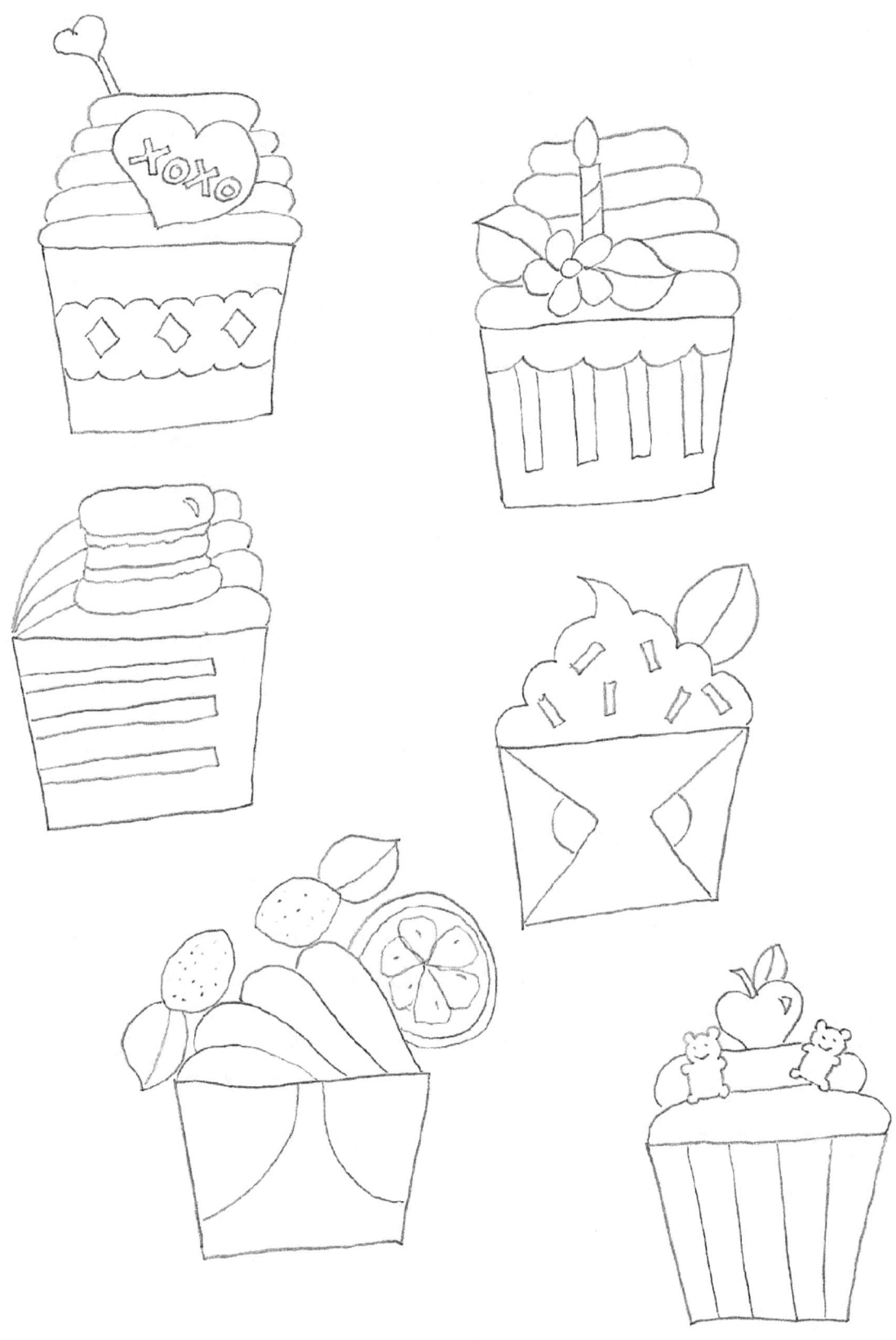

THANK YOU FOR PURCHASING MAGICAL DESSERTS VOLUME 3 COLORING BOOK. IF YOUR CHILD ENJOYED THEIR COLORING EXPERIENCE, YOU MIGHT FIND MY ADULT COLORING BOOKS INTERESTING FOR BOTH YOU AND YOUR CHILD. THE BELOW BOOKS CAN BE PURCHASED AT AMAZON.COM:

VINTAGE PARIS BAKE SHOP (Adult)

VINTAGE WINE GARDEN (Adult)

ICE CREAM MADNESS (Adult)

ICE CREAM MADNESS VOLUME 2 (Adult)

TEA & COFFEE TROPICAL TREASURES (Adult)

TEA & COFFEE OCEAN TREASURES (Adult)

TEA & COFFEE TREASURES (Adult)

BOTANICAL FLOWERS & MANDALAS (Adult)

MAJESTIC FALL (Adult)

FAIRIES IN THE FLOWER SHOP

MERMAIDS' WONDERLAND SEA OF ENCHANTMENT

A VERY RETRO CHRISTMAS (Adult)

MAGICAL DESSERTS (Children)

MAGICAL DESSERTS VOLUME 2 (Children)

FASHION DOLLS (Adult)

CHRISTMAS DESSERTS (Adult/Child)

IF YOU ENJOYED YOUR COLORING EXPERIENCE, PLEASE TELL OTHERS ABOUT IT BY WRITING A REVIEW ON AMAZON.COM UNDER THE BOOK YOU COLORED.

www.ingramcontent.com/pod-product-compliance
Lightning Source LLC
Chambersburg PA
CBHW080132240526
45468CB00009BA/2370